ACTION

ASK THE EXPERTS

WEIGH THE EVIDENCE

BE A SKEPTIC, NOT A CYNIC

MAKE SURE IT'S NOT A JOKE

USE FACT-CHECKING RESOURCES

STICKING TO THE FACTS

10 Ways to Fight Misinformation

GREGOR CRAIGIE

illustrated by

BITHI SUTRADHAR

ORCA BOOK PUBLISHERS

ORCA TAKE ACTION!

For everyone who wants to know the truth.

Published in Canada and the United States
in 2026 by Orca Book Publishers.

Library and Archives Canada Cataloguing in Publication
Title: Sticking to the facts : 10 ways to fight misinformation / Gregor Craigie ; illustrated by Bithi Sutradhar.
Names: Craigie, Gregor, author | Sutradhar, Bithi, illustrator.
Description: Series statement: Orca take action ; 3 | Includes bibliographical references and index.
Identifiers: Canadiana (print) 20240174170 | Canadiana (ebook) 20240174189 | ISBN 9781459840416 (hardcover) | ISBN 9781459840423 (PDF) | ISBN 9781459840430 (EPUB)
Subjects: LCSH: Misinformation—Juvenile literature. | LCSH: Disinformation—Juvenile literature. | LCSH: Fake news—Juvenile literature. | LCSH: Media literacy—Juvenile literature. | LCSH: Information integrity—Juvenile literature.
Classification: LCC P96.M4 C73 2026 | DDC j028.5—dc23

Library of Congress Control Number: 2025933432

Summary: Part of the nonfiction Orca Take Action series for middle-grade readers, this illustrated book gives young readers tools to spot fake news and actions to take to fight misinformation and disinformation.

Orca Book Publishers is committed to reducing the consumption of nonrenewable resources in the production of our books. We make every effort to use materials that support a sustainable future.

Orca Book Publishers gratefully acknowledges the support for its publishing programs provided by the following agencies: the Government of Canada, the Canada Council for the Arts and the Province of British Columbia through the BC Arts Council and the Book Publishing Tax Credit.

Cover and interior artwork by Bithi Sutradhar.
Design by Troy Cunningham.
Edited by Merrie-Ellen Wilcox.

Printed and bound in South Korea.

29 28 27 26 • 1 2 3 4

CONTENTS

> Truth exists. Only lies are invented.
>
> **Georges Braque**, painter

NOTE: Fake news can also appear in newspapers and magazines, but in this book we'll focus mainly on what we find online.

Introduction

There's no shortage of information available online. Photos, videos, memes, stories, facts and figures are all just a click or swipe away. And more information is available every day, as millions of us post on an ever-growing list of digital platforms.

But not all of that information is trustworthy. Some of it contains mistakes. Some of it is downright wrong, even though it claims to be right. We call this fake news—false information that is made up and shared to mislead or deceive others. I've been a journalist for more than 25 years, and in that time I've seen fake news become more common and grow into a much bigger problem for all of us.

There are two broad types of fake news. Misinformation is false or misleading information that's shared without intending to deceive. In other words, misinformation is wrong, but probably not wrong on purpose. On the other hand, disinformation is intentionally designed to deceive. It can be shared to make people develop opinions that the writer wants them to believe. Both misinformation and disinformation are huge problems.

So how do we know what's real and what's fake? And how can we fight fake news? This book will help! The fact is that we can all learn to spot fake news and take action to stop its spread. And that's the truth!

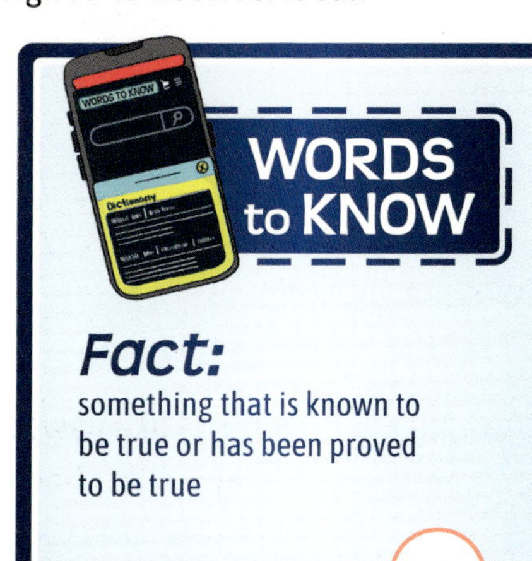

Fact:
something that is known to be true or has been proved to be true

ACTION ONE

Consider the Source

WORDS to KNOW

Source:
in journalism, a person, publication or record that provides the information that you read in a news story

News Organization:
a group of people that gathers information and then shares it with the public through the internet, newspapers, radio, television and other forms of mass communication

Hoax:
a widely seen joke or trick that is designed to convince many people that a false story is real

When we scroll through search results or the headlines on a news website, it's often the subject of the story that catches our attention and makes us click on the article. We are interested in what is happening. But we should pay just as much attention to where the story comes from—the source—as we do to the story itself.

WHO'S RESPONSIBLE?

The first thing to check is the organization that hosts the website and its history. For example, if you find an interesting article about mountain gorillas on the *National Geographic* website, you are reading a report from an organization that has been around for more than 130 years, reporting on interesting stories from around the world.

national geogr

On the other hand, if you click on a headline about giant monkeys who have invaded New York City and taken over the Empire State Building, and it takes you to, say, www.giantmonkeysinvadeNYC.net, you probably shouldn't believe the story. (I made up that URL, so it definitely wouldn't be a trustworthy source!)

Just because *National Geographic* has been around for a long time doesn't mean it never makes mistakes. In fact, it has made plenty of mistakes over the years. More important, it's not only willing to admit to its mistakes but willing to correct them too.

But what if you don't know whether to trust a website? There are a few things you can do.

OOPS!

A 2023 article about the collapse of the Maya civilization incorrectly stated that the ruins of an ancient city, called Piedras Negras, are located in northeastern Mexico. But that's not true: the site is actually located in northeastern Guatemala. You can read about this on a page called "Corrections and Clarifications" on the *National Geographic* website.

LOOK for "ABOUT US" and a BYLINE

First, look for "About Us," usually at the top or the bottom of a website. It should explain the purpose of the website and list the people who work and write content for the website.

Next, does the story have a byline stating the author's name at the top or bottom of the page? And is there a link that tells you something about the author? Knowing something about the author can help you decide whether you can trust what you're reading. (We'll take a closer look at that in the next chapter.)

Facts are stubborn things; and whatever may be our wishes, our inclinations, or the dictates of our passions, they cannot alter the state of facts and evidence.

John Adams, second US president

COMPARE and CONTRAST

Another important way to check if a news website is reliable and has a good reputation is to compare what it says with what a different website or news organization says about the same subject. But make sure you compare it with a reputable organization, like *National Geographic*, that you already trust. That doesn't mean the two websites should report exactly the same thing or have the same opinion. But it's a good way to see if the website you're checking is sticking to the basic facts.

Before you believe something you read online, find out something about the website and who operates it.

Read what other websites or authors say about the same story.

GOOD TO KNOW!

A ***fact*** is something that is known or proven to be true. Journalists are taught that they can provide the facts for their readers by answering five or six fundamental questions, often called the five W's:

WHO? WHAT? WHEN? WHERE? WHY?

(There's sometimes an additional question: **How?**)

FAMOUS FAKES

THE GREAT MOON HOAX

In 1835 a newspaper called the *New York Sun* published six articles describing the discovery of alien life on the moon. These sensational stories appeared to be written by a scientist named Dr. Andrew Grant. They described unicorns, two-legged beavers and human-like creatures with bat wings. "They averaged four feet in height," one article claimed, "were covered, except on the face, with short and glossy copper-colored hair, and had wings composed of a thin membrane, without hair, lying snugly upon their backs, from the top of the shoulders to the calves of the legs."

The newspaper quoted a famous astronomer to make the stories sound true and claimed the articles were reprinted from the *Edinburgh Journal of Science*, which had been a real publication but had stopped publishing a few years earlier. But all of it was pure fiction. The stories were written by the newspaper's editor, Richard Adams Locke.

So what was the goal of printing these stories? Money! The newspaper was only two years old, and its owners wanted more paying subscribers, which it got, thanks to these stories. A few months later, the editors admitted that the moon story was a hoax. But it didn't seem to hurt the *New York Sun*, which was to stay in business for another 115 years.

THE SUN

Check the Author

When we read an article or watch a video, we're almost always interested in *what* it's about. But we should also pay careful attention to *who* created it. Finding out about the author is another important tool we can use to identify fake news.

WHO WROTE the STORY?

Is the author named? And if they're named, are they a real person? Many supposed authors of fake news are made-up people who don't exist. Or the name used in the article isn't the name of the person who wrote the article. In some cases, someone simply makes up a name and uses a stolen photograph of someone else. It isn't hard to do. There are billions of images online, and it only takes a few clicks to copy and paste them.

WORDS to KNOW

Journalist: a person who writes news for websites, magazines, newspapers, radio or television

Nonprofit: a group or organization operated for a community, public or social benefit—not to make money for owners

Reverse image search: use of a photo, without text, to search for information online

ARE THEY QUALIFIED?

If the author is named and they are a real person, the next question to ask is whether they are *qualified* to write the story.

For instance, are they a journalist whose job it is to interview people, do research and write clear articles to help the public understand what's going on? If they are a journalist, look at other articles they've written. Have they written other articles on the same subject? Have they written about the subject for a long time? If the answer to these questions is yes, it's a good sign that the journalist knows a lot about the subject.

Of course, the author doesn't have to be a journalist. Maybe they're an expert in the field—someone who has in-depth knowledge about a subject, usually through a combination of experience and education—like a doctor writing about childhood traffic injuries, or a police officer writing about the dangers of speeding drivers.

But authors don't have to be experts. Sometimes the best articles come from what you might call "regular people" with something important to say. Maybe they have direct experience with the issue in their day-to-day life, like someone who writes an article about the need for flashing lights over crosswalks after seeing a pedestrian being struck by a car.

You can check to see if a photo is real or fake by using an online reverse image search tool, like Yandex or Google Reverse Image Search. If you find the photo used with many different names, it's probably a fake. We'll look at some of the specific apps and websites you can use to find fakes in **ACTION EIGHT.**

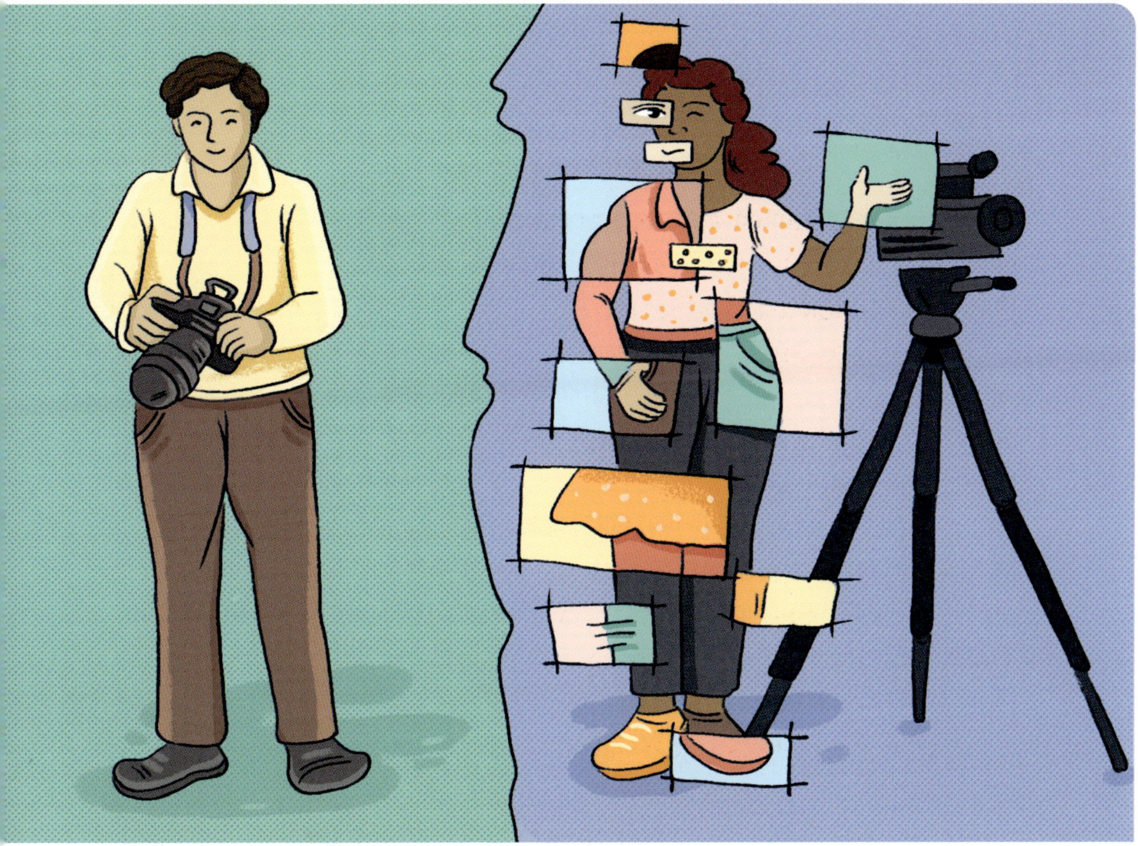

A QUESTION of TRUST

It's not always possible to learn whether an author is real or trustworthy. But with time you'll come to know some authors you trust, based on reading several articles they have written. That doesn't make them perfect. It just means you're willing to read what they write, and think about it carefully, before making up your mind.

what YOU can DO

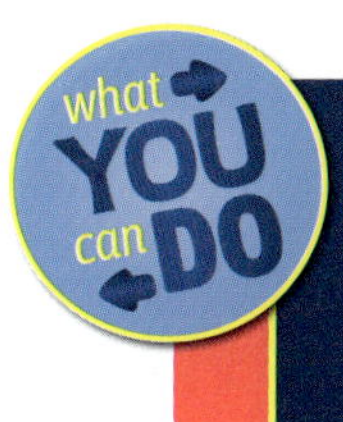

Find out who wrote the story.

If there's a photograph in the article, do a reverse image search on it to see if it's a fake.

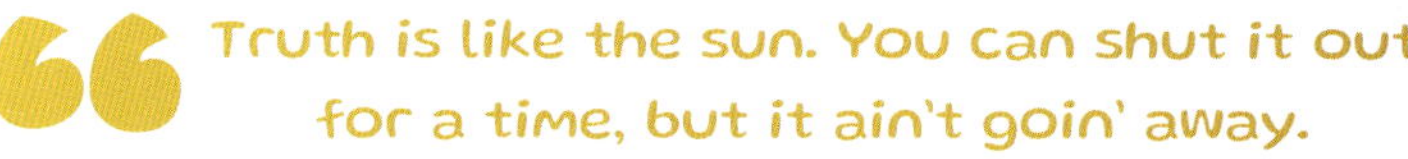

> Truth is like the sun. You can shut it out for a time, but it ain't goin' away.

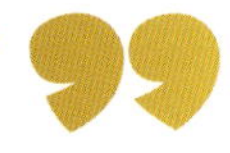

Elvis Presley

USING DISINFORMATION AGAINST WOMEN IN POLITICS

When Ukrainian politician Svitlana Zalishchuk gave a speech to the United Nations in 2017, she wanted to tell the world how the ongoing military conflict between Russia and Ukraine was affecting women. She spoke passionately about their suffering and said the fighting with Russia had shifted the focus for most Ukrainian women from fighting for equality to fighting just to survive.

But almost as soon as Zalishchuk had finished speaking, a fake post on the Twitter/X social media platform claimed she had promised to run naked through the streets of Ukraine's capital, Kyiv, if Russian-supported soldiers won an important battle in eastern Ukraine. This was completely untrue—but that didn't stop it from spreading far and wide, circulating on the internet for a year. "It was all intended to devalue me and what I'm saying," Zalishchuk lamented.

The Brookings Institution, a nonprofit government research group, says this kind of online disinformation, which targets women, makes it more difficult for women to succeed in politics and is a significant reason why many women abandon political careers. So it's all the more impressive when women in politics fight back to help fight fake news. Zalishchuk joined with other concerned Ukrainians to form a nonprofit organization called StopFake that works to stop false online news stories and encourage international efforts to fight disinformation.

Read Past the Headline

ACTION THREE

It may sound obvious, but when we read an article online, we should read the *whole* article. We need to go all the way to the end! A lot of people don't. Some don't even read past the headline.

Headlines have to be short so they can fit in a small space on your screen. They almost never tell the whole story, even if they're correct. And sometimes they're not correct at all. They may be sensational or provocative on purpose to get more people to click on the link so the website will get more money from advertisers. Even reliable news organizations sometimes get headlines wrong, especially if the person who wrote the article didn't write the headline.

The more that you read, the more things you will know. The more that you learn, the more places you'll go.

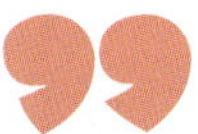

Dr. Seuss

Satire: the use of humor, exaggeration or ridicule to criticize the actions or opinions of someone else

THE GOLDEN RULE OF SHARING

If you're not sure, don't share! Many articles include different perspectives on a subject, especially if it's controversial or still being debated. If you read only the headline or a few sentences, you might miss different points of view or opinions. So think and read before you share. And if you don't understand something, or you know it's not true, don't share it.

LIFE IS COMPLICATED

It's important to remember that many issues are really complicated, and they can't be summed up in a headline or even in one or two sentences. So you need to keep reading to properly understand the issue that's being written about.

Here's an example. In 2020 a number of headlines left readers wondering if there might be alien life on the planet Venus. "Astronomers Find Possible Sign of Life on Venus," was the *CBS News* headline. "A Possible Sign of Life Right Next Door to Earth, On Venus," was *NPR*'s headline. While neither of these headlines was wrong, both could create the impression that aliens exist in our solar system.

In reality, scientists had detected traces of a rare molecule, called phosphine, which is created by microorganisms here on Earth. That led scientists to wonder if the phosphine on Venus might have been created by microorganisms. Scientists didn't know if that was the case or not, and both articles made that clear. But you would only understand that by reading past the headlines.

Read the whole article, not just the headline or other parts of it.

Remember the golden rule: share something only if you're sure it's true.

FAMOUS FAKES

POPE ENDORSES TRUMP

Four months before the 2016 American presidential election, online news reports claimed that Pope Francis had declared his support for the Republican candidate, Donald Trump. That would have been quite the story, not only because millions of Roman Catholics listen carefully to what their leader says, but also because popes have long been careful *not* to endorse candidates.

In fact, that was still true in 2016—the pope didn't support any candidate. So how did the story get all that attention?

It turns out that it first appeared on a fantasy and satire website, no longer online, called *WTOE 5 News*, which published fictional stories and made itself look like a US television station website. It openly admitted to publishing fake news, stating: "Most articles on wtoe5news.com are satire or pure fantasy."

In its report on Pope Francis and the presidential election, the website claimed that "news outlets around the world" were reporting the pope's unusual endorsement. That wasn't true either. No reputable news organization reported this story because the pope didn't endorse *any* candidate.

In a press conference, Pope Francis made it clear: "I never say a word about electoral campaigns." But that didn't stop the story from being shared and shared and shared. By the time voters cast their ballots in November, it had been seen nearly one million times on Facebook.

ACTION FOUR

Weigh the Evidence

WORDS to KNOW

Perspective:

a person's specific attitude toward or opinion about something—their point of view

Editorials, op-eds and opinion pieces:

articles that share an opinion on a subject and are designed to persuade readers to agree with the author

Witness:

a person who has seen an event, like a crime or an accident, take place

Meteorologist:

a highly trained scientist who studies Earth's atmosphere, oceans and land surface and looks at how they affect weather conditions

Most responsible news articles provide more than one perspective on a subject. There are a few exceptions to this rule. But articles that we read to find out *what actually happened* should check with several people.

A GOOD AUTHOR ASKS MORE THAN ONE PERSON

An article doesn't always have to include several perspectives on a subject. But life is complicated, and some things can be both good and bad, depending on whom you ask. So an author who wants to be fair should ask more than one person.

For instance, an article about an unexpected spring snowfall should explain how it affected different people. It could include quotes from frustrated truck drivers who couldn't deliver groceries to a supermarket because the roads were closed. It could also feature photos of happy kids sledding down snowy hills one last time before summer arrives. If the article only shows frustrated drivers, it makes the storm look like a bad thing. If it only shows happy kids, it makes it seem fun.

Asking several people also reduces the risk of getting things wrong. A good author will check with many different people to confirm that what they're writing actually happened. If the author asks only one person what happened, their article will be more likely to contain errors than if they had asked two people. Or 10.

Education is education. We should learn everything and then choose which path to follow.

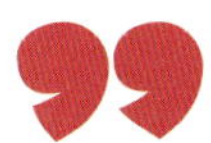

Malala Yousafzai, activist and Nobel Peace Prize laureate

CONSIDER A DIFFERENT POINT OF VIEW

Even if you agree with an article that doesn't include any other perspectives, search for more articles on the subject and try to find one with at least one different point of view! You may not like what an article says, but it's important to know what other people think.

WHERE'S the PROOF?

In addition to having more than one perspective, a good article will have *proof*. It will explain the available facts or information that show whether something is true.

It can be a quote from someone with direct knowledge of the story—someone like a witness or an expert. In that big spring snowstorm, the witness could be a driver who describes how they were stuck in traffic for two hours, and the expert could be a police officer who reports that there were dozens of minor car accidents in less than an hour.

Evidence can also be simple facts or statistics. Maybe it's a meteorologist who looked at the satellite data to confirm that the big spring storm dumped more snow on the city than any other storm in the last 50 years. The evidence in an article is what should convince you that what you're reading is true—or not.

If you're still unsure about the reliability of an article, see if the author is backing up what they write with facts. Click on any links in the article. Does the author quote anyone? Is there more than one perspective?

Read articles that quote more than one person.

Ask yourself if the author has any evidence to prove what they say in the article.

FAMOUS FAKES

SWENEKAFEW!

In 1903 reporters and editors at the *Clarksburg Daily Telegram* were spitting mad at the rival newspaper in their West Virginia town. They were convinced that the *Clarksburg Daily News* was stealing their stories. But they didn't have any proof. So they made up a fake news story—on purpose!—to get it.

The *Daily Telegram* published a fake news story about someone they called Mejk Swenekafew, who the paper reported had been shot at a local coal mine. The story said the man was shot by someone he knew, after the two men had a fight about a dog. It described many details of what happened, even though none of them actually took place and none of the people in the story actually existed. Every word of the story was fiction.

The day after the article about Mejk Swenekafew was printed in the *Daily Telegram*, a similar story appeared in the *Daily News*. That was all the evidence the staff at the *Daily Telegram* needed to catch their competitor in the act. If anyone doubted it, all they needed to do was look closely at the name Mejk Swenekafew. If you spell Swenekafew backward, it reads, *We fake news!*

The copycat *Daily News* had just printed proof that they were stealing stories. As the *Daily Telegram* reported to its readers, "The *Daily News* has been caught fair and square in its nefarious work!"

ACTION FIVE Ask the Experts

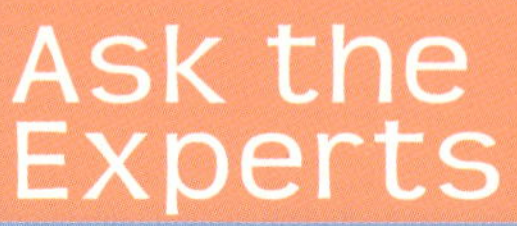

WORDS to KNOW

Reliable: of high quality and can be trusted, time after time

Extreme: goes far beyond the normal limits that most people consider reasonable or acceptable

Sometimes a story is too complicated to make sense of on our own. For example, if an article says the world is getting warmer and links the changing climate with extreme weather events like heat domes and massive wildfires, how do we decide if it's true or not? One option is to ask an expert.

WHY ASK an EXPERT?

An expert can answer your questions.

Let's say you've just read that story about climate change and still have questions about it. Maybe you wonder how we know that human activity is heating the planet, and whether every storm or flood is caused by climate change or if it's just weather. Who can you ask?

A great place to start would be to ask a meteorologist. They analyze data from satellites, weather balloons and radar systems to try to predict weather events that might be days or weeks away, like hurricanes, tornadoes and thunderstorms. They also study how weather patterns change over the years and how human activities, like burning coal, affect those patterns. In other words, a meteorologist is an expert on climate change.

> The only thing you absolutely have to know is the location of the library.
>
> Albert Einstein

LOOK for a LIBRARIAN

If you're still not sure whether something you've read is real or fake, you can always ask an expert at finding answers—a librarian. Librarians are information experts!

They do a lot more than help you find books. They can help you find multiple different sources, from digital databases to e-books. You could think of school librarians as navigators of new information—they won't tell you *what* to think, but they'll show you *how* to find reliable answers from people who have a real understanding of the issues that interest you.

Most of us may not know a meteorologist personally. But a lot of news organizations have meteorologists who can answer your questions. In fact, for some of them it's a part of their job. Their email is often listed on the organization's website.

what YOU can DO

Listen to people who have studied something for many years.

Go to the library if you need to look for more answers.

FAMOUS FAKES

THE CHANNEL SWIM HOAX

On a cool fall evening in 1927, Dorothy Cochrane Logan waded into the cold ocean water at Cap Gris-Nez, France. The English doctor loved to swim and had plenty of experience swimming long distances in cold ocean waters. She covered herself in black axle grease, to keep her body warm, and put on her goggles before starting her swim across the English Channel under a moonlit sky. When she walked out of the water on the beach at Folkestone, England, 13 hours later, it looked like she had both broken the world record and earned £1,000 from a British newspaper (worth more than $10,000 today).

But it soon emerged that she had spent only four hours in the water and another nine hours on a boat, seasick and wrapped in a blanket in a small cabin belowdecks. Logan claimed she had cheated on purpose—to prove how easy it was to fool the world and to show that contests like this one needed people supervising to make sure no one cheated.

This sounded fishy to the newspaper's writers and readers. Asked about it by a journalist, one of the people who had accompanied Logan insisted that she had only confessed to cheating because he'd demanded it. Others believed Logan and pointed out that she had never cashed the check. Either way, she got neither the money nor the world record.

Teachers can often help you find information too!

Pay Attention to the Date

ACTION SIX

Some stories aren't wrong or misleading intentionally—they're just old! Most news websites leave articles online for many years. That can be okay if we read an article as a record of what was known when it was written. It can be really useful because we often need to check what things were like in the past. But when we read an article that was written several years ago as though it were information about what's happening *now*, it can cause problems.

A lie gets halfway around the world before the truth has a chance to get its pants on.

Winston Churchill, British prime minister during World War II

WORDS to KNOW

Context:
the information or circumstances around an event or idea that need to be known to fully understand the event or idea

OLD NEWS ISN'T NEW NEWS

Treating an old article as though it's new is different from fake news, but it's still misleading. That's because things change over time, and what might have been true in the past isn't necessarily true today.

Imagine it's a scorching-hot summer day, and you read an article telling you to wear wool socks and a warm sweater. You wonder if the author wants you to collapse from heat stroke. But then you discover that the article was written six months ago, just before a major blizzard! When something is taken out of context like that, its meaning is changed, and people can be misinformed as a result.

Here's a real-life example. In 2019, when a giant fire broke out in Notre Dame cathedral in Paris, the fire made headlines around the world. Several Facebook pages started sharing an old, unrelated news story from 2016 about a car that was discovered near Notre Dame with gas canisters inside and a note written in Arabic. Some misinformation experts believe the older story was shared on purpose by someone who wanted to make it look like the 2019 fire was started by someone who was Muslim. Investigators would later say the fire was started by either a cigarette or a short circuit in an electrical system.

WHEN WAS IT WRITTEN?

So what can you do to fight this possible source of misinformation? The answer is pretty simple: check the date! It's usually below the headline and before the first words of the article. That's not always the case, though—after all, if an article explains how to boil an egg, we don't really need to know when it was written! But a news story needs to have a date.

Some articles will be updated after they were first written, and responsible authors and organizations will include that information as well.

Always look at the date on which an article was written or a video was produced.

If it's old news, consider how things might have changed since then.

FAMOUS FAKES

GORDON LIGHTFOOT'S NON-DEATH

Gordon Lightfoot was a world-famous musician in the 1960s, called Canada's greatest songwriter by many entertainment writers and music lovers. So in 2010 when online news reports that he had died started to spread like wildfire, radio stations across Canada and the United States started sharing the news that was circulating online and playing some of his most famous songs.

But Lightfoot wasn't dead at all. He was sitting in a dentist's chair! After the appointment, he turned on the radio and got the shocking news. "I was quite surprised to hear it myself, driving into my office," he later said with a laugh. "I haven't had so much airplay for weeks!" Lightfoot had been the victim of a death hoax, a deliberate report of someone's death that is later found to be untrue.

A friend of Lightfoot's, the rockabilly legend Ronnie Hawkins, said he had received a phone call from a man claiming to be Lightfoot's grandson, who told Hawkins the sad (fake) news. "Oh, what a dirty, sick joke that was," Hawkins said. "But I'm glad it was a sick joke and not the truth."

Finding out exactly where the sick joke started is tricky, but a spokesperson for Gordon Lightfoot believed it began on the social media platform Twitter, now known as X. Lightfoot kept on singing and performing for many years. He died in 2023 at the age of 84.

Some news organizations now try to avoid confusion by adding a notice to articles 12 months or older that reminds readers the information might be out of date. Those notices appear on their websites, and they also appear when the story is shared on social media.

Make Sure It's Not a Joke

Speaking of jokes, most of us like to laugh. It can be good for us, both physically and mentally. Jokes can also bring welcome relief when we feel overwhelmed by bad news. But we need to know that a joke is a joke and not a real news story. Unfortunately, that isn't always the case. There are plenty of examples of online jokes that have been mistaken for real news.

IT HAPPENS EVERY YEAR

The problem often spikes on April 1—April Fools' Day—when people play practical jokes. This is nothing new. In fact, the April Fools' Day habit of playing tricks on people has been popular for centuries. But it's become even more popular in the internet age—people make up jokes and put them in fake news articles that are *supposed* to be false. That's part of the joke, and the author or organization will eventually make that clear, usually before the end of the day.

Before they do, though, they want to fool readers into thinking the joke is real, and every April 1 some people mistake a prank for real news. And because so many online articles stick around for a long time, many people mistake them for real news many months or even years after they were first posted as a joke.

APRIL FOOLS!

In 2015 toilet-paper company Cottonelle tweeted that it would start making toilet paper for left-handed consumers. It was an April Fools' joke, and it fooled a lot of people, who shared it online.

AN OLD ONE, but a GOOD ONE

In 1980 the British Broadcasting Corporation (BBC) reported that Big Ben, the iconic clock tower in London, would have its beautiful, ornate clock-face replaced with a giant digital readout. Many listeners recognized the story as a joke, but lots of others thought it was real, and they complained. The BBC apologized. But the joke has been repeated many times in recent years and shared widely on social media by people who believe it's real.

April Fools' Day has proved extremely popular over the years, and that's not likely to change. It doesn't usually cause problems if the people reading the jokes realize they're jokes, not facts. So if you read something that seems really hard to believe, check the date!

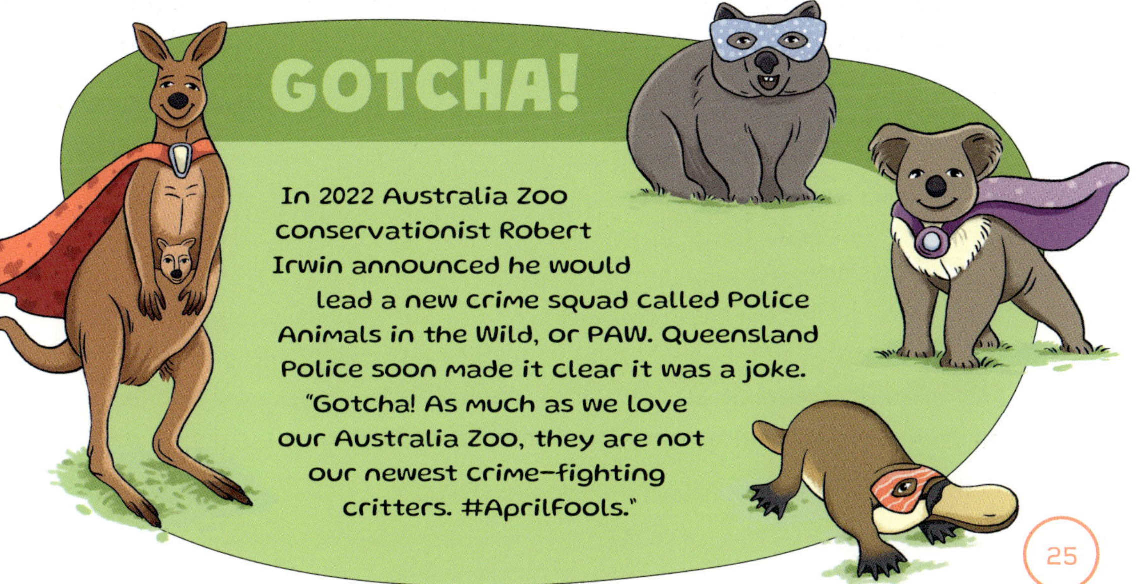

GOTCHA!

In 2022 Australia Zoo conservationist Robert Irwin announced he would lead a new crime squad called Police Animals in the Wild, or PAW. Queensland Police soon made it clear it was a joke. "Gotcha! As much as we love our Australia Zoo, they are not our newest crime-fighting critters. #AprilFools."

Check to see if an article was written on April 1.

Ask yourself, Is it too ridiculous to be true?

FAMOUS FAKES

NO MORE NAKED ANIMALS!

The headline certainly caught the world's attention. "*National Geographic* to Stop Publishing Nude Animal Pictures." The story was shared widely on social media and featured a very cute photo of a prehensile-tailed porcupine, a type of porcupine that lives in trees in Central and South America and is covered in short, multicolored quills that give it a speckled appearance. The porcupine in the *National Geographic* post was holding its two front paws in front of its midsection, looking almost bashful, as if embarrassed because it wasn't wearing any clothes.

It wasn't unusual for *National Geographic* to post a high-quality photo of a wild animal. But the headline about naked animals just didn't feel right to many people reading it. Sure, we should treat animals with respect. But they don't wear clothes! It's not, well, natural.

"Sooo..." one reader posted on *National Geographic*'s Facebook page, "does this mean we'll be seeing animals with a sweater and a pair of jeans in future *National Geographic* magazines? Animals have 'clothes'...called fur and hair." Many readers posted similar comments about the strange article.

But other readers noticed something else. A clue. The date at the top of the article was April 1, 2016. "Woops..." another reader posted, "someone didn't get the April Fool's memo?"

A day without laughter is a day wasted.

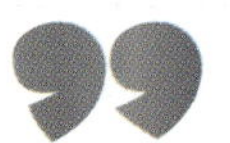

Charlie Chaplin, comic actor and director

Use Fact-Checking Resources

ACTION EIGHT

If you're not sure whether something you read is true, and you can't find an expert to ask, you can search for answers on an online fact-checking website that's designed to do some of the sleuthing for you. Here are two examples.

Fraud:
the crime of deceiving people for financial or personal gain, or illegally interfering in an election

Transcript:
a printed version of the exact words someone said

Artificial intelligence (AI):
technology that uses computers to copy human intelligence and learn without being programmed by people to perform specific tasks

Fan fiction:
stories written by a fan of a particular TV series, movie or entertainer

POLITIFACT

PolitiFact reviews questionable claims in American politics. For example, a 2024 post on the social media platform Threads claimed that President Donald Trump said he would build a national "iron dome" missile system to defend America against missile attacks from Canada, if he won the election later that year. The post was liked more than 2,000 times. But it was only partially correct—Trump *did* promise he would build an iron dome, but he did *not* say it would protect the United States from Canada.

The website has also corrected false statements made by Trump. One of those was his frequently repeated claim that he didn't really lose the 2020 election to Joe Biden but was the victim of fraud. *PolitiFact* said this was wrong: "Trump's own advisers, federal and state officials, and judges nationwide found no widespread fraud in the 2020 election." The article's sources included more than a dozen articles, social media posts, emails and transcripts of Trump's speeches.

There are many online tools to help, but sometimes you just can't be certain. If that's the case, remember the golden rule for fighting fake news: if you don't know it's true, don't share it.

There's so much active misinformation and it's packaged very well and it looks the same when you see it on a Facebook page or you turn on your television...if everything seems to be the same and no distinctions are made, then we won't know what to protect.

Barack Obama, 44th US president

SNOPES

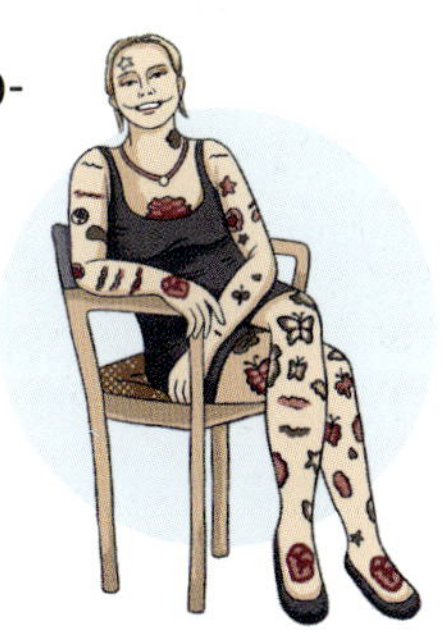

Another popular fact-checking website is *Snopes*. It was established in 1994, when the internet was nearly brand-new. *Snopes* investigates questionable stories on a range of issues, from a story that actor Kristen Bell had 214 tattoos (she doesn't have any) to a claim that a person can survive by eating a diet of only potatoes and butter (they can "survive," but they would be extremely unhealthy).

One of the reasons readers trust *Snopes* is that its authors admit when they don't know if a story is true or not. If they don't have enough evidence, *Snopes* marks a story either "undetermined" or "unverifiable."

FACT-CHECKING PHOTOS

Sometimes it's not the words you want to check but the photos. What if you think someone has changed a photo or a video? Or used an artificial intelligence (AI) program like Sora to create short video clips that look real?

Fact-checking websites like *FotoForensics* let you upload photos or videos to find out if they're real, and some offer tutorials to help you identify more fake images in the future.

Use a fact-checking website to find out whether something is true.

Take an online tutorial on how to spot fake images.

FAMOUS FAKES

BILLIONAIRE WEDDING

In 2017 a photo of two young women wearing long, flowing dresses went viral. It was in a story claiming the two women were Chinese billionaires who had just been married and become the world's richest couple.

The story wasn't true. Meng Mei Qi and Wu Xuan Yi were actually part of a 13-member K-pop band called Cosmic Girls (also known as WJSN), with members from South Korea and China. They didn't get married. And although their band was popular and made a lot of money, they weren't billionaires.

The hoax appears to have started as a joke in a tweet from a fan that was retweeted more than 20,000 times, leading many people to believe the story was true. The photo also helped convince many people that the story was true. The women's dresses, one white and the other cream-colored, looked a lot like traditional wedding dresses.

But the K-pop stars weren't at a wedding. They were sitting side by side on a couch at the Beijing International Film Festival. The original photo, first posted by Wu Xuan Yi on Weibo, a popular social media site in China, included two men, one on either side of the women. The men had been cropped out of the tweeted photo.

Even when the real story came out, some Cosmic Girls fans said it should not be called "fake news" but should be considered fan fiction instead. What do you think?

Be a Skeptic, Not a Cynic

ACTION NINE

A skeptic is a person who doubts something they hear but who is willing to believe it's true if they are shown convincing evidence. In contrast, a cynic is someone who is not willing to believe what they're told. A skeptic is a doubter. A cynic is a disbeliever. That distinction may sound like a small thing, but it makes a big difference.

I KNOW THAT I KNOW NOTHING

The ancient Greek philosopher Socrates was famous for being skeptical. He said, "I know that I am intelligent because I know that I know nothing."

SKEPTICS

The English word *skepticism* traces its roots to the Greek word *skepticos*, which means "to find out" or "to inquire." A skeptic is a critical thinker who doesn't simply believe what they are told but considers it carefully before deciding if it's true.

It's important to note that skeptics don't simply choose to think that what they're reading is a lie. In many cases a skeptic will believe and trust, but only after considering different arguments and evidence. A skeptic is also willing to change their point of view based on the facts. A skeptic has an open mind.

WORDS to KNOW

Media: the different forms of mass communication, information and entertainment, such as the internet, social media, TV, radio, magazines and newspapers

CYNICS

A cynic, on the other hand, is someone who has a closed mind. The *Oxford English Dictionary* defines a cynic as "a person who believes that people are motivated purely by self-interest rather than acting for honorable or unselfish reasons." As a result, they tend to focus on what's negative—and usually expect the worst. They are not willing to believe there might be other explanations for something bad that happened, such as the possibility that it was just an accident.

Being cynical means you are much less willing to change your mind, if you are willing to change it at all.

SO WHAT?

So why does this distinction between skepticism and cynicism matter?

It's good to have a healthy amount of doubt—to be a skeptic—about things you hear or read, to not believe something simply because someone else says it. This makes you less likely to be fooled by a lie or mistake. It also means you've thought about the things you know and believe, but you're still willing to change your mind if the evidence supports that.

Meanwhile, a cynic won't change their mind and is unlikely to believe anything they hear or read. The cynic is certain that everyone else is wrong.

Be a critical thinker—but also be willing to change your mind.

> There is nothing so pitiful as a young cynic because he has gone from knowing nothing to believing nothing.

Maya Angelou, poet

> Cynicism masquerades as wisdom, but it is the farthest thing from it. Because cynics don't learn anything. Because cynicism is a self-imposed blindness, a rejection of the world because we are afraid it will hurt us or disappoint us. 
>
> **Stephen Colbert**, comedian

FAMOUS FAKES

THE DEATH OF MARK ANTONY

Fake news has been around for thousands of years. It was used in 30 BCE, when the Roman Republic was on the brink of a civil war between Octavian, the adopted son of the great general Julius Caesar, and Mark Antony, one of Caesar's top military commanders.

Antony was a formidable fighter, so Octavian chose a different type of weapon to win the war—misinformation. He started a fake news campaign that claimed Antony was always drunk, didn't respect traditional Roman values and had a romantic relationship with Cleopatra, the Egyptian queen, who Octavian claimed was controlling Antony.

Mark Antony and Cleopatra did love each other, but a lot of what Octavian claimed was either questionable or untrue. So how did Octavian spread this fake news 2,000 years before the internet? He used one of the most common media of the day—coins! If this seems like a strange way to share a message, just think about how often coins are shared.

Octavian wrote short, catchy, false phrases about Antony and had them engraved on coins. On other coins, he showed himself wearing a laurel wreath above the words *Libertatis Populi Romani Vindex* (avenger of the freedom of the Roman people).

Octavian's misinformation campaign convinced many Romans to support him. Antony's soldiers were defeated in the Battle of Actium, and Octavian was crowned as the first Roman emperor.

LIBERTATIS POPULI ROMANI VINDEX

Look in the Mirror

ACTION TEN

No one is perfect. We all make mistakes. One of the things that leads us to make mistakes is something called bias, which is a preference for an idea, person or thing that is based on our personal opinions, which may be inaccurate, prejudiced or unfair. We all have bias, whether we know it or not. It doesn't make us bad people. In fact, it's natural.

WORDS to KNOW

Prejudiced:
having a preconceived opinion that is not based on reason or actual experience

Silo:
a tower or an underground chamber. The ***silo effect*** is what happens when people stick with people who share the same beliefs and viewpoints and isolate themselves from people with different ideas.

CHECK YOUR OWN BIAS

How can you make sure you don't believe fake news simply because you *want* to believe it? First, you can accept that you have biases. Then you can take some time to ask yourself some questions. The questions will probably be a little different for everyone, but they could be about who you are more inclined to trust. For example:

AM I MORE INCLINED TO BELIEVE SOMEONE WHO LOOKS LIKE ME?

DO I NATURALLY TRUST SOMEONE WITH THE SAME SKIN COLOR AS I HAVE?

DO I TRUST SOMEONE WHO IS THE SAME GENDER AS ME OR SPEAKS THE SAME LANGUAGE?

If the answer to any of these questions is yes, keep that in mind the next time you doubt something said by someone who doesn't look like you.

None of this means it's wrong to have opinions, thoughts and beliefs. They're an important part of who you are! But almost all of us, no matter what we believe, will be better informed if we consider different perspectives.

 There is only one corner of the universe you can be certain of improving, and that's your own self. 

Aldous Huxley, writer and philosopher

WATCH OUT for SHARED BIASES

You might also share certain biases with a lot of other people, like a bias in favor of tall people. In his book *Blink: The Power of Thinking Without Thinking*, Malcolm Gladwell looked at the chief executive officers, almost all of whom were men, of top American companies and found that 30 percent of them were at least 6 feet, 2 inches (188 centimeters) tall, yet only 3.9 percent of American men were that tall.

It's hard to say exactly what's behind this, but it's likely our society has an unconscious bias that associates tall people with natural leaders. But I think we should push back against this thinking. As someone who is taller than almost everybody I know, I can tell you that being tall doesn't make someone a better leader!

STOP the SILO EFFECT

You can do more than just identifying your own biases. You can let other people challenge them as well. That doesn't mean you have to spend all your time getting into arguments, but you can have respectful conversations with people who have different points of view.

This is really important in a time when social media platforms separate us into different silos, where we see and hear a lot of people who agree with us but few who have different opinions.

Be honest with yourself about why you want to believe or not believe something.

Accept that you have biases and that everyone else does too.

FAMOUS FAKES

A BAN ON MOTORBIKES THAT WASN'T

Alexandria Ocasio-Cortez was elected to the US House of Representatives in 2019. New Yorkers who voted for her liked her views on social issues and the environment. Her opponents claimed she had radical views on things like climate change, and some were willing to believe an online article claiming that Ocasio-Cortez wanted to ban motorbikes from the United States in an effort to cut pollution.

The article said she wanted to create a "nationwide motorcycle ban." It even included a made-up quote attributed to Ocasio-Cortez: "And I'm supposed to slow my Prius down so you can, like, noise pollute past everyone?"

But the whole thing was fiction. It was published on a website called *Taters Gonna Tate*, where the "About Me" page states, "Everything on this website is fiction. It is not a lie and it is not fake news because it is not real. If you believe that it is real, you should have your head examined."

Still, the article was shared more than 6,000 times on Facebook. And even though Facebook flagged it as part of an effort to combat fake news and misinformation, some readers believed it was real. One wrote, "Back off!!! A good majority of motorcyclists are retired veterans. She is NOT going to be able to do it." Of course, the truth is that she had no intention of doing it.

Resources

Links to external resources are for personal and/or educational use only and are provided in good faith without any express or implied warranty. There is no guarantee given as to the accuracy or currency of any individual item. The author and publisher provide links as a service to readers. This does not imply any endorsement by the author or publisher of any of the content accessed through these links.

PRINT

Delisle, Raina. *Breaking News: Why Media Matters.* Orca Book Publishers, 2023.

Grant, Joyce. *Can You Believe It? How to Spot Fake News and Find the Facts.* Kids Can Press, 2022.

Holzer, Hannah Rose. *TIME for Kids: Kid Reporter Field Guide: A How-To Book for Junior Journalists.* Penguin Young Readers Licenses, 2024.

McKee, Jonathan. *The Teen's Guide to Social Media...and Mobile Devices: 21 Tips to Wise Posting in an Insecure World.* Barbour Publishing, 2017.

Yasmin, Seema. *What the Fact? Finding the Truth in All the Noise.* Simon & Schuster Books for Young Readers, 2023.

ONLINE

Dealing with Propaganda, Misinformation and Fake News: coe.int/en/web/campaign-free-to-speak-safe-to-learn/dealing-with-propaganda-misinformation-and-fake-news

Fighting Misinformation: Why Pausing Before You Share Really Works!: mediasmarts.ca/fighting-misinformation-why-pausing-you-share-really-works

How to Avoid Falling for Misinformation and Conspiracy Theories (*Washington Post*, July 15, 2024): washingtonpost.com/technology/2024/misinformation-ai-twitter-facebook-guide

Preventing the Spread of Misinformation and Disinformation: rtdna.org/preventing-the-spread-of-misinformation-and-disinformation

What Is Misinformation and Disinformation? torontopubliclibrary.ca/misinformation-and-disinformation/index.jsp

Acknowledgments

Thanks first and foremost to Merrie-Ellen Wilcox, who did such a fine job editing this book, and to Kirstie Hudson, who has edited my other nonfiction books for Orca Books and who asked me to write a book about misinformation. I'm also grateful to everyone else at Orca who helped with this book: copyeditor Vivian Sinclair, proofreader Brock Peters and, of course, illustrator Bithi Sutradhar, whose wonderful images bring my words to life. I'm also thankful to the many journalists I've worked with in different newsrooms—at BBC, CBC, CBS, PRI and CKWX. Over the years I've been inspired by countless colleagues who work tirelessly to find the facts and share the truth with the public.

Index

CLARKSBURG DAILY NEWS
SWENEKAFEW SHOT!
CLARKSBURG DAILY TELEGRAM
MEJK SWENEKAFEW KILLED IN SHOOTING!

LIBERTATIS POPULI ROMANI VINDEX

TO BAN MOTORCYCLES

JUST MARRIED: WORLD'S RICHEST COUPLE.

WHAT CAN

A BETTER FUTURE FOR EVERYONE STARTS WITH

GOOD ALLIES:

1. SUPPORT THOSE WHO DON'T HAVE THE SAME PRIVILEGES.
2. ARE WILLING TO CONTINUALLY REFLECT, LISTEN AND LEARN.
3. UNDERSTAND THAT ALLYSHIP ISN'T EASY OR COMFORTABLE.

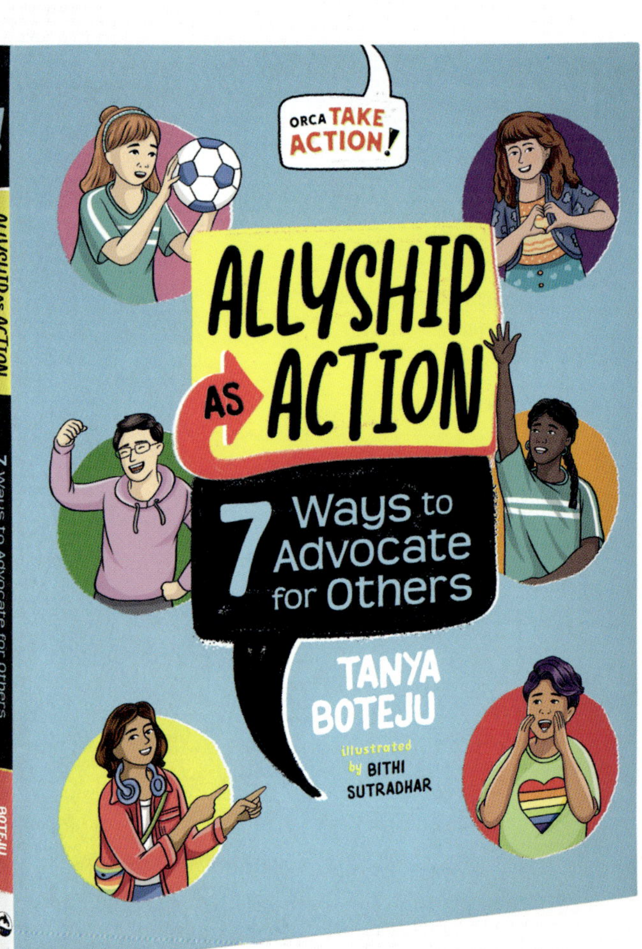

Being an ally is about learning and action. It's hard work, but everyone can be an ally. Explore definitions of allyship, privilege, marginalization and more, and work through realistic scenarios to develop tools to be best ally you can be.

YOU DO?

helps you understand important issues and shows how you can make changes.

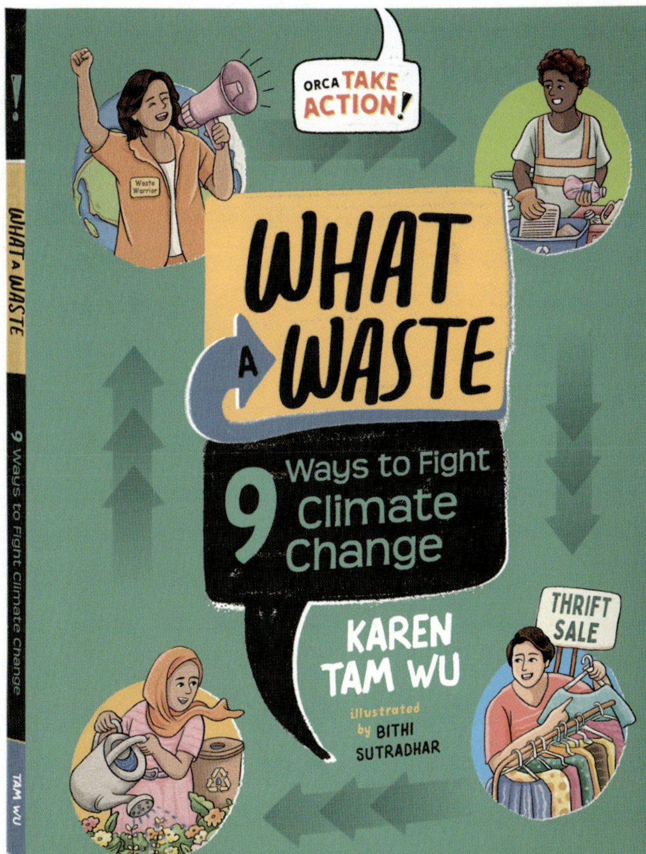

Our garbage doesn't have to be trash. Waste can be a resource and tool to help the planet. Discover cutting-edge projects and actions you can take to reuse and repurpose garbage.

WASTE WARRIORS:

1. FIND WAYS TO REDUCE OR REUSE PLASTIC.
2. REPAIR DEVICES BEFORE REPLACING THEM.
3. BUY SECONDHAND CLOTHES OR ORGANIZE CLOTHING SWAPS.

Rebecca Craigie

GREGOR CRAIGIE is a writer and journalist. He has worked in radio for more than 25 years at the Canadian Broadcasting Corporation and the BBC World Service in London. He wakes up at 3:45 every weekday morning to talk on CBC Radio in Victoria, British Columbia. Despite the early hours, Gregor loves his job because he gets to ask questions and write for a living. He has written several books for adults and children.

BITHI SUTRADHAR is a Bangladeshi illustrator and graphic designer who holds a master of publishing degree from Simon Fraser University, as well as an MFA and BFA in graphic design from the University of Dhaka. Alongside her professional illustration work, Bithi enjoys sharing her knowledge and skills through teaching. Her contributions have been recognized by educational institutions and government bodies such as the Ministry of Agriculture in Bangladesh. In 2024, Bithi created the illustrations for the first three books in the Take Action series as part of an internship with Orca Book Publishers. Bithi lives in Vancouver and loves exploring the vibrant outdoor scenes in her spare time, finding inspiration in the city's natural beauty.

Anik Saha

TAKE

CONSIDER THE SOURCE

PSST!

PAY Atten-tion TO THE DATE

READ PAST THE HEADLINE

LOOK IN THE MIRROR

CHECK THE AUTHOR